BOOKS BY PHILIP LEVINE

1933

1933

POEMS BY

PHILIP LEVINE

NEW YORK   ATHENEUM   1974

I thank the editors of the following magazines in which these poems, often in earlier versions, first appeared:

AMERICAN POETRY REVIEW (*Goodbye, Hold Me*)

THE AMERICAN REVIEW (*Once in May*)

ANTAEUS (*Harvest*)

ATLANTIC (*Uncle, The Name of the Air*)

FIELD (*1933*)

HUDSON REVIEW (*Late Moon, War*)

IOWA REVIEW (*Zaydee*)

IRONWOOD (*Grandmother in Heaven*)

KAYAK (*First Love, 1945, After*)

THE NEW YORKER (*Going Home, Ruth, The Poem Circling Hamtramck, Michigan All Night in Search of You*)

THE OHIO REVIEW (*No One Knows the Yellow Grass*)

POETRY (*I Am Always, Losing You, One by One, I've Been Asleep, Bad Penny, Death Bearing, Letters for the Dead*)

TRANSPACIFIC (*At the Fillmore*)

In memory of my father

and in praise of my mother

who gave me these words

CONTENTS

I

ZAYDEE

Why does the sea burn? Why do the hills cry?
My grandfather opens a fresh box
of English Ovals, lights up, and lets the smoke
drift like clouds from his lips.

Where did my father go in my fifth autumn?
In the blind night of Detroit
on the front porch, Grandfather points up
at a constellation shaped like a cock and balls.

A tiny man, at 13 I outgrew his shirts.
I then beheld a closet of stolen suits,
a hive of elevator shoes, crisp hankies,
new bills in the cupboard, old in the wash.

I held the spotted hands that passed over
the breasts of airlines stewardesses,
that moved in the fields like a wind
stirring the long hairs of grain.

Where is the ocean? the flying fish?
the God who speaks from a cloud?
He carries a card table out under the moon
and plays gin rummy and cheats.

He took me up in his arms
when I couldn't walk and carried me
into the grove where the bees sang
and the stream paused forever.

He laughs in the movies, cries in the streets,
the judges in their gowns are monkeys,
the lawyers mice, a cop is a fat hand.
He holds up a strawberry and bites it.

He sings a song of freestone peaches
all in a box,
in the street he sings out Idaho potatoes
California, California oranges.

He sings the months in prison,
sings salt pouring down the sunlight,
shovelling all night in the stove factory
he sings the oven breathing fire.

Where did he go when his autumn came?
He sat before the steering wheel
of the black Packard, he turned the key,
pressed the starter, and he went.

The maples blazed golden and red
a moment and then were still,
the long streets were still and the snow
swirled where I lay down to rest.

GRANDMOTHER IN HEAVEN

Darkness gathering in the branches
of the elm, the car lights going home,

someone's beautiful Polish daughter
with a worn basket of spotted eggs,

an elbow of cabbage, carrots, leaves,
chicken claws scratching the air,

she comes up the cracked walk to the stairway
of shadows and lost dolls and lost breath.

Beautiful Polish daughter with hands
as round and white as buns, daughter

of no lights in the kitchen, no one sits
on the sofa, no one dreams in the tub,

she in her empty room in heaven
unpacking the basket piece by piece

on the silent, enamelled table
with a little word for each, a curse

for the bad back and the black radish
and three quick spits for the pot.

I AM ALWAYS

I

I sit on the toilet, the lid down,
the room misted with steam.
My father talks and sings by turns
of the power of machine guns
no man can face, of a home home
on the range. Money is what
they want, he says, and more
and a way of keeping it.

He stands before the mirror
running the thick white towel
between his legs, and then dries
carefully the long root
half hidden in hair. Black tufts
sprout under the arms, black
crosses the chest, and a shadow
cuts across the hard belly.

I I

I lie naked on the metal table
where they must have brought
my father. There's nothing wrong,
the Doctor says, nothing
I can find. He's too frail,
mother says. No.
He's growing. He'll become
a man. They all do.

I shut my eyes
and see my own legs stretching off
like peninsulas, my chest
and stomach bursting with rocks,
groves, fields of tall grasses
with black pools of water underneath.
I keep them shut. Even the stars
exploding won't open them.

III

I am always a boy swimming up
through the odors of beer and dreams
to hear my name shivering
on the window. Beside me mother
curls on her side, a bare round arm
under her head, her hair unwound
fans out, her mouth half closes
around the words I can't hear.

The floor is cold. I dress quickly
pulling up the high socks first
and then the knickers, and carry
the shoes out to the kitchen.
Outside by the scaling backyard fence
a boy in a gray cap calls me out,
his long hands deep in his pockets
hiding the dark thumbs and bitten nails.

THE NAME OF THE AIR

They would arrive late
because of the rumor of war
and move slowly, fearing
the Lord in a Whirlwind
who hovered always above
U.S. 24. They ate
everything and drank steadily
and were never drunk.
The gifts they left
weren't here in the morning
nor were they, who left
somewhere near the end
when the cake collapsed,
the rug smouldered,
and the dances choked. They
are here in my hand, faceless
in the sudden flash, bowing
to sunlight or turning in a smear
of shade, thumb prints
on an oily knife, and so pass
to the future to breathe
only when I breathe and lightly
not to distress the smoke
and stain the brow of
the woman in white and the man
in black, holding hands,
who turn suddenly away
from each other to stare
into the twin eyes of darkness
or read this first time
the name of the air.

LOSING YOU

Another summer gone.
the hills burned to burdock
and thistle, I hold you
a moment in the cup
of my voice,
you flutter
in the frail cave of the finch,
you lean to speak
in my ear
and the first rains blow
you away.

Dusk is a burning
of the sun.
West of Chowchilla
The Lost Continent of Butterflies
streams across the freeway.
Radiators crusted,
windshields smeared with gold
and you come on
rising into the moons
of headlights.

My brother is always a small bear,
cleaning his paws,
I am a leopard
running through snow,
you are the face of an egg
collapsing sideways.
Now the last olive falls
gripping its seed
a black stone among stones
and you are lost.

In a white dress
my little girl goes to the window.
She is unborn,
she is the thin flame
of a candle,
she is her mother
singing a song.
Her words frost
the mirror of the night,
a huge wind waits
at the back of her breath.

I'VE BEEN ASLEEP

The last warehouse closes down
banging its iron lids
from the sagging pipes a river begins
drop by drop
running over the paws of mice
my mother dreams: her shiny purse
is empty at last
she goes to the open window
and laughs

In the morning
things are not the same
a long vein of lettuce unclenches
the earth, squash trumpet
their blossoms at the sun
the onions are higher
coming into their purple crowns

smears of dust
hang over the hills
where the trucks wound down
bringing home their cartons of silence
I lean forward slowly
into water
my hands lifting me into cold water
slipping between my fingers

ONCE IN MAY

Once in May the earth seemed
all there was, all
there had to be, and I waited
at the sea's edge not counting
anything, and after a while
walked in, my white pants darkening,
my shirt going soft, fountain pen,
billfold, letters, notes,
small change all slipped away
and I was no one, a boy
laughing at the hidden stars,
a boy jeered by a mob
of Spanish boys. I stood
all afternoon under heaven
with water in my pockets,
salt in my socks, naming
the grains of the sea
and blessing the kids,
until the face of the waves
deepened and the winds came
shuddering in and I huddled
under a blanket and sang.
The moon rose slowly
showing its broken face,
the ring of stars climbed
to the tips of my fingers,
one bright planet crowned my hair
and hummed until dawn.
The sea gray and sliding,
small boats coming in,
the men tired, gray, unloading
hake, merluza, squid in handfuls,
sea bass, prawns, sword fish,
great finned flat fillets,
the cold meats of the deep.

BAD PENNY

After the Peace of Ghent
he took the streetcar
half way home, transferring
at Grand Blvd. The sky
hung just above the elms
and now and then a star
broke through. Near dawn
after the last cigarette,
a warm wind and the snows
hushing, wind tugging
at his long coat.
He started to walk.

The school yard silent,
the first green
shining through, the pond
he skated once, small,
gray with floating curls
of newspaper. He climbed
the fence, heaving up
and over. Block after
block of brick flats
and nothing moving until
a cardboard suitcase
spilled its tripe
in the snow.
                I turned
to say *What happened*
or *Our Father*
but he was gone,
the streetlight dimmed
in the first flush of day,
the star gone.

★

After I die
go out and dig all morning
in the garden working,
your scarred hands
down through the light loam
until you find that root
like wood, like the four
walls of my life,
until you find
the bad penny I paid
the earth, and rub
its face for luck
and shine it with spit
until it glows again.

HARVEST

My mother could lie down
under these gnarled
trees, sleep
for a moment and rise
with the wisdom
of ripe fruit circling
a stone. She saw
the earth darken
around a rose, heard
the wind knock
and she opened.

I see the Angel of Death
lean from his cab
and spit blood. I go
into the day, my hands
behind my back, all
the secrets of life out
on the counters among
the jades and zircons.
The afternoon wrinkles.
Next door the widow
in a new kimono, her blue
veined ankles bare,
carries out the garbage.

Snow grays by
the back fence, mice
blacken under leaves
rabbits freeze
on the runways and the lights
come on. Money is all,
we say. The cat steps out
the back door into the night,
her pockets empty,
and breathes the rich harvest
of the alleys.

II

ONE BY ONE

One by one
the lights appear at sea,
not the stars drowning
as they must, but small boats
—*Dolores, Dragon Boy,*
St. James of the Heights—
orange and scarlet hulls,
unblinking eyes
and bared teeth flashing
on the prows. All afternoon
they steamed on the sand
and the fishermen dozed
in the buzzing shade and woke
blinking in the first
chill winds. Now
in the deepening rose
of day's end, they slide
into the breakers and bob out
to meet the moon.

★

By the open window
a woman making stew,
her hair falling in her eyes
black strand by strand.
The bare bulb pulsing
like a nerve sparkles
on her little moustache
of sweat. Banging
on the worn board
her blade slashes
the hides of 12 potatoes
6 carrots 4 onions
2 turnips 8 tomates
and 1 deep root
the power of

which will reduce us
all to angels. Singing
she dips a flour-whitened
forefinger in, licks
it dry, and turns
the fire down.

*

The barracks asleep
just before dawn,
out back
two soldiers who walked
the long way in.
They sling their carbines
on the wash pole,
remove their green capes
and the thick tunics
under them. In the darkness
pale chests splotched
with hollows
and clumps of hair,
long arms shivering,
they work the pump
bowing by turns
to the black stream,
rubbing the cold water in
to neck and eyes and brow,
and cursing their mothers.

LATE MOON

2 a.m.
December, and still no moon
rising from the river.

My mother
home from the beer garden
stands before the open closet

her hands still burning.
She smooths the fur collar,
the scarf, opens the gloves

crumpled like letters.
Nothing is lost
she says to the darkness, nothing.

The moon finally above the town.
The breathless stacks,
the coal slumps,

the quiet cars
whitened at last
Her small round hand whitens,

the hand a stranger held
and released
while the Polish music wheezed.

I'm drunk, she says,
and knows she's not. In her chair
undoing brassiere and garters

she sighs
and waits for the need
to move.

The moon descends
in a spasm of silver
tearing the screen door,

the eyes of fire
drown in the still river,
and she's herself.

The little jewels
on cheek and chin
darken and go out,

and in darkness
nothing falls
staining her lap.

WAR

At noon my sister
comes home in a cab
she stops on the landing
embracing a sack
of groceries and looks back
she's lost her new stockings
and her black gloves
somewhere she's
been awake for days
she fumbles in her purse
feeling the dark wads
of money

Before the sink
she cries in the half light
shaking out the yellow chips
sinking her hands
slowly in water
twisting and untwisting
the two slips
she stares out
the bathroom window
the ore boats dark
against the Canadian shore

Later the radio argues
and she falls asleep
on the sofa
the kettle steams and steams
the windows go black
she dreams her husband
is home, his fists burned red
he wants his children
and will have them
she wakens believing
her life is over

She tells herself
she will sleep again
and waken with another man
in another life
she tells herself
this war will end
when she can
no longer stand it
the way the rain ends
when a jar
overflows on the sill
she tells herself
she must be strong
so her mother
will kiss her
so the two slips will dry

        ★

December 1942
a bleeding soldier in a torn jacket
waits at the back of a diner
no one asks him anything
dead horses blaze in the cold, wheels
lock, crates of secret wings slide forward
in the guarded hallways children stand
for hours holding their metal trays
downtown the workers sleep in the movies
their heads hung back over the seats
their mouths wet and calling
when the darkness spreads from the factories
oiling everything, they waken
not as the ghosts of women
black and white, dancing in tears
but as themselves and go out
into the streets past the beer gardens
where the sisters burn like salt
and they remember nothing

FIRST LOVE, 1945

March and the snows have turned—
perhaps the war is over—
the gray crust gives
under their weight
and small rivers sigh
in the streets.
Coming home
from the dance
where no one danced, he's
in love with Polly Basil.
Holding her hand
does nothing for it,
breathing beside her
the moon-drenched air,
letting the silence speak
of the slow weight
in his belly
does nothing for it.
Against the chain-link fence
going for throat and ears,
breast and crotch,
helps a little.
Hours later she loses her hankie
under the viaduct,
this is love,
his shoes darken
like small struck animals.
The rails above
shudder and gasp under
frozen wheels. A light oil
runs on his back,
runs on her lips and cheeks,
runs on everything,
on bitten ears
that hear too much,
on tongues of machines

that never stop,
on the one eye
of the star
that winks them to their beds.

AT THE FILLMORE

The music was going on.
The soldier paced outside
his shoes slowly filling

with rain. Morning
would walk early
over the wards of the wounded,

row after row
of small white faces
dragged back.

She dozed in the Ladies
wondering should she
return. This warmth

like the flush of juice
up the pale stem
of the flower, she'd known

before, and its aftermath—
seeing the Sisters
and the promises again.

The music was going on,
a distant pulsing only
from the wilderness of strobes.

He climbed back up
the crowded stairs cloaked
in a halo of rain, and no one

noticed or called.
Nor were those the waters
of the heart she heard

rushing in the booth
beside her. She stubbed
her cigarette and rose.

The music was going on
gathering under
the turning lights, mounting

in the emptying hall
toward the end. They stood
blinded a moment,

and then she offered herself
to his arms and opened
her arms to him, both

of them smiling as they
claimed the other
and whatever else was theirs.

RUTH

They would waken
face to face, the windshield
crystaled, the car
so cold they had to get out.
Beyond the apple orchard
they saw where the dawn sun
fell among plowed fields
in little mounds of shadow
and a small stream ran black below
where the rocks slept.
Her wrists pounding
against it, she rubbed
the water into eyes
and temples, the iron taste
faint on her tongue.
And they'd get going, stopping
for cokes and gas
and cold candy bars all
through Ohio,
and when the sun failed
north of Toledo
they were almost there,
the night sky burning
up ahead at River Rouge
like another day.

Another day.
Now he was gone, the children
grown up and gone
and she back home,
or whatever you could call it,
West Virginia.
A wafer of sunlight
on the pillow, and she rose
and heard the mice startled
beneath the floorboards. Washed
in the sink, lit the stove,

and waited. Another day
falling into the fields, tufted
like a child's quilt.
Beyond the empty yard
a wall of poplars stared back,
their far sides
still darkness, and beyond,
its teeth dulled with rust,
the harrow tilted
on one frozen wheel, sliding
back to earth.

NO ONE KNOWS THE YELLOW GRASS

My friend and I climbing.
Along the trail smears
of yellow, baby tufts
tousled by wind, here
and there putting out
white faces.
Pebbles slipping away
under our boots, starting
the long walk back to salt.
By noon we were there.
On a treeless shelf
out over nothing, we stopped
to look and talk
and came back down
a different way, between
great hunched shoulders
of granite. In the cold
of the high pines I found
the last of a cat,
hard and gray, the sockets
swimming with ants, the jaws
clamped on a smile
as though they'd swallowed
the earth.
                    When I got back
I asked his woman
what were they called
by mountain people.
Jump-ups. No, I said
I knew jump-ups,
and took her out
past the chicken house
in a cold wind
the both of us shivering
our faces still red

out across the road
and half way up
the steep hillside
under Black Mountain
and pointed to
a ribbon of yellow grass
in the twisted winter shade
of the oak. Hell,
I don't know, she said,
and turned and spit
and shuffled back to the stove.

GOING HOME

She brought oranges
in a basket
of woven broom.
I brought briars,
thistles, thorns,
and the long silences
of the road. Cross-legged
on the bed, she mended
socks, put back
the lost buttons
biting off the thread
with a smile.

I wakened
in the darkness
and talked
to the darkness,
remembering
the cities, the first
weeks without work,
rain falling
afternoons
in the gray rivers,
the women staring.

First light
paled the windows
and she wakened.
We rose quickly
and dressed.
She walked me
to the highway, leaping
ahead over
field pools
and through the bent grass
her skirts lifted.

THE POEM CIRCLING HAMTRAMCK, MICHIGAN ALL NIGHT IN SEARCH OF YOU

He hasn't gone to work,
he'll never go back to work.
The wife has gone home, mad,
with the baby on one arm.
Swaying on his good leg,
he calls out to the bare bulb
a name and opens his arms.
The old woman,
the beer gone from her glass,
turns back to the bar.
She's seen them before
with hard, knotted bellies,
with the bare white breasts of boys.
How many times has she stared
into those eyes glistening
with love or pain
and seen nothing
but love or pain.
Deep at night, when she
was coldest, he would always
rise and dress so as not
to miss the first streetcar
burning homeward, and she
would rock alone toward dawn.

If someone would enter now
and take these lovers—for they
are lovers—in his arms
and rock them together
like a mother with a child
in each arm, this man
with so much desire, this woman
with none, then it would not be
Hamtramck, it would not be

this night. They know it
and wait, he staring
into the light, she into
the empty glass. In the darkness
of this world men
pull on heavy canvas gloves,
dip into rubber coats
and enter the fires. The rats
frozen under the conveyors
turn to let their eyes
fill with dawn. A strange star
is born one more time.

DEATH BEARING

The sun wakens staining her pillow
in the bathroom the bowl has yellowed
her son is gone

A pale spider scurries into the lightbulb
and flares like hair

The child is gone in the cup of coffee
he is gone in the cigarette

The lips of the snapdragon are soft and full
the bluejay caws out his crest

He is gone in the white folded napkin
gone in the reflections of the knife

The young plum tree straightens in the wind
dust settles on the lids of the grape

He is gone in her shoulders
gone in the small black hairs curling
on the backs of her fists

     ★

She closes her eyes

In the middle of a dry field
a child dies like an ark
nettles burn
darkened grasses, late wildflowers
We run away to the edge
and there turn to look
We come back step by step
holding the immense heat in our eyes
We hear the animals inside
the bears calling for water, the horses

lying down in the straw
the lion praying
The crib is on fire
the gray roof takes wing and flaps off
the windows are sugar
running into dark pools

          ★

She cannot wait for death to leave
the basin steams
she washes the tiny shirts
shaking out the least trace of death
she wrings the hankies into which death cried
under the bed she finds the two socks
in which death frolicked
she heats the iron against death
her hand grazes a cheek down which death rained

A hand is luminous against the noon
five fingers each with its five deaths
each nail dying into a moon
and the moons waning
All these hands that work for death

She wants a small boy
his arms around her neck, his cheek
roughing hers
they are singing his little poems
they are planting bright flags in the air
they run out of breath

III

LETTERS FOR THE DEAD

The air darkened toward morning
the slag heap's yellow flame
paled against the sky

on the sill the old wren
slept till noon   I wakened
read the paper

and thought of you one by one
and tried to hold your faces
in my eyes

tried to say
something to each of you
of what it is
without you

the winter sun
dipped below the stacks
the chilled tea whitened
in my cup

*

The drug store fired your mother
she dried and hardened

the butcher never returned
to beat his soft palms
against the door

his stiff coveralls hung in the closet
your briefcase
bulged with rusting tools

your shoes aged
the toes curling upward
in a spasm

your voice, your high voice
of pear and honey
shuddered once along the bare walls

but someone ate the pear
someone ate the honey
—we still ate at the usual hours

and went off to the factories in the dark
with bloodless sandwiches
folded in wax paper
with tiny packages of sweets

no one felt your sleep
arriving
or heard the sudden intakes of fear

no one held your hands
to keep them still
or your face glowing like a clock's

at night the toilet ran
a window hummed in the wind
your final letter uncrumpled to the moon

when your father came home at last
drunk repentant eager to beg
there was no one to answer

the salt scattered on the table
untasted

★

On south past Toledo
the bus heading into the great oven
into your first adventure

a man is chewing
a man is lying about love
a frightened corporal loads
and unloads a .45

your face against the black glass
unlined, forever young

out of the miles
of breathing fields suddenly
a small white town
locked against the night
with one light burning

then the cities
the bus hot
and filling with silent
black men

no women anywhere
squad cars hunched on the corners
waiting for life
on past the dark barracks
rail yards
all-night car lots
the last bar winking

At Covington the pale Ohio
inches toward the sea
the bridge gathers its nerves
and you cross
holding your breath the whole way

the dawn of a new world
it grays
climbing the first hills
and up over the grinding ridges
turning slowly to stone
the roadside trees fighting
for light

Later, slate waves
at Pensicola
you stood
and counted them
and turned for home

—The clock silent in the shrunken parlour
the cold plate waiting

     ★

She dyed her hair black
circled her eyes with blue moons

he drank beer and more beer
till morning splotched his face
his eyes puffed shut

the doctors reworked her face
the mirrors clouded
so she lay with anyone
turning toward the wall
to cry

outside the freezing church
through half the night
his lips soft and pink
as a girl's
he lay down in snow
scratched at trees
tore into his own arms

himself a child
he turned from his children
to shake his fist
in his own face

she married and unmarried
flushed and aborted
she wrote
The jar that stood so high
broke
and fell away
she showed the words to everyone

he whispered into the dead phone
I'm from Dearborn and I'm drunk

They were all we had
of you before the car
shuddered a moment
then faced the coming traffic
all we knew of you
before the siren's pulsing faded
and the white attendant
turned and lit a cigarette

★

3 a.m.
Early April and the house chants
in the night winds
each window gives back
a face
the lie is retold in the heart
the old denials burn
down the hallways of the brain
the dead refuse to die

the air crackles with their angers

the young mother wakens suddenly
and flees her bed and her own children
running over the mountain ground
her old man choking on his lungs
demands to be heard
the aunt paces the closed room
the brother burned in Asia
howls like a tree

And the children die
the sacraments we waited for
go gray
little flat sacks of refuse
and no one can look
or look away

the father, enormous
bunched against the green wall
says
over and over
Can you believe we loved you

All night
rain in the still river
off the loading docks at Wyandotte

locked wheels
blind eyes of cars
the scattered intestines of purses
a pale carp
warped on its side

they bump slowly underwater

       ★

When will the grass be bread
when will the sea winds bring no salt
to raze the yellow shoots
the pear grind its sand
honey sting the tongue
when will the stars put out their eyes
our hands touch
and the onion laugh

Above Three Rocks
40 miles from here sheep gather
in the mountains
huddling together
in a cup of earth and stone
until a bud of light
flowers in the east
and the old Basque with a cane
comes to lead them down
the passes

       ★

The sea calmed
the village darkened toward dawn
I was there

47

awake in a strange room
my children
breathing slowly in the warm air

down the hall
the workers bunched together
three to a bed grunting
in sleep

beside me my wife
in still another world

on the roof
not a single light
the sea reflecting
nothing
one black wave untipped
with spray
slipping toward shore
to spread like oil
—and then no more

nothing moved
no wind
no voice
no sound of anything
not one drop riding down my face
to scald the earth

★

I ate an apple
the skin the sour white meat
the core
how I relished
the juice

Praise the apple

I struck my strange tall son
again and again
until my wife came begging
from our bed
and pulled me away

for 40 days
I dreamed my death like yours
at great speed
the bones shattering into meat
blood blurring the world
the spirit issuing outward
in a last breath

and came to land
weak and alive
the sunlight crossed my bed
I rose and fed the cat
the green worms fattened
on the vine
I looked in the corners
of things

high on my brother's left shoulder
I carved the old scar
again and again
my signature cut
almost to bone
even the brown silky hairs
and the mottlings from birth
will never hide it

Let the scars shine

south of Cadiz
I stopped the car and ran
in winter mist
to the black margin of the world
the wet rocks stared out unseeing
my tracks crumbled behind me

Bless our blind eyes

      ★

Early March
a clear and windy day
in the village of Fuengirola
near the new concrete housing project

the workers playing soccer
on their noon break

under a torn roof of rushes
he sat in shadow
legs crossed

a tiny man burned by sun
unshaven for days
a campesino I'd seen
many times coming home
his corduroys dusty
in the first dark
one special Sunday
bearing
a gleaming sea bass
gaffed and dripping
down the length of one leg

a small stiff man
now bowing forward to strike
his forehead against the earth
the left hand flung out
and opened to the sky
the right hand bunched
to his breast

hidden below the cries of play
the words I couldn't understand
the strikings of the earth
again and again
the shakings of the head
NO NO
the eyes riding in tears
seeing and unseeing
the mouth asking everybody and nobody
Why Why

until the trees blackened
the air chilled
the oil drums flared
a moment
and died
wind sound only
bamboo creaking through the cold night
and by morning he was gone

tending his patch of lettuce
combing the small field
of fine green onions
stooping all day
to the parched earth

★

No one comes home from school
above the porch
the light takes hold

the papers bleed in a puddle
all night the radio
jives itself

a photo torn in half
dances in the grate
like a cry for help

your books on the shelf
give up their words
one by one

your wedding band
with its secret calligraphy of wear
sleeps in a coffee can

a turnip forgotten
darkens
at the back of the drawer

the mice
settle in the walls
their fierce hearts ticking

Morning—
on the freeway
a white cap skips
and I slow for an instant
and pass

warm days—
the child you never saw
weeds the rhubarb
white grains collect above his lips
and flake away in the sudden wind

even the dead are growing old

IV

AFTER

After the fall of the tree
the ants came out to see the sun pass
to the Kingdom of Shadows

After the water bled
the toad grew a shell
and held still

After the wren pierced her eggs
after the snake went to sea
the clouds rusted
and wept in snow
no one could explain

After her husband died
she said, He's gone away
he was here in his heavy bed

The milk stayed neutral
the Turk made a round sandwich
and ate in the light
the broom lay down with the dust

After the windows were locked
and the front door
I found chips of smoke
in my little drawer of shirts

The old auntie screamed
in the shop of white stones
with her little gloved fists
she beat the wheel of our car
we left her the flowers the trees
the cold grass the afternoon of rain
that goes on and on

Again at dawn I come home
to my head on this pillow
the coverlet frozen
the fingers hidden, home
to a name written in water

GOODBYE

Waking to silence
all the beds empty and made
but mine.
A long autumn morning
the shades drawn past lunch,
the house cool
and quiet, grandmother shushing.
I rode a worn sofa
silently into battle
lashing my flanks.
In the kitchen
uncles and cousins strange
in their serious suits
and shirts, holding
their hands on the table.
The bathroom too warm
and full of smoke, smoke drifting
blue and heavy
in the last cracks of light
long after everyone had gone.

Mama sat
in the living room
in the dark
in the big chair.
She said,
"The good die young"—
not to me or anyone.
It was Mama
with long black gloves
coming out her sleeves
and a black fox
stiffening at her throat.

★

The grass was stiff
and springy, bright green
with yellow and brown spears
burned underneath.
Underneath the willows
I was tired and asked
to lie down in the shade
but had to go right up
to the long dirt hole
red in the sunlight
and say, Goodbye.

Later, beside a still pond
of white ducks
Grandpa sat
and cleaned out my ears
with a white hankie and a match;
he held my face back
in his little speckled hands
and said,
"Your nose is dirty too."

When the woman slid
down on the wet grass
Grandpa took an amber jar
to her nose until she shook
her hair loose
and her eyes rolled open
and she bit her mouth.
The ducks drifted off
under the wooden bridge.
Grandpa said
the baby ducks were
where the children went.

★

In the first light
a sparrow settled outside
my window, and a breeze woke
from the breathing river,
I opened my eyes
and the gauze curtains
were streaming.
"Come here," the sparrow said.
I went. In the alley below
a horse cart piled with bags,
bundles, great tubs of fat,
brass lamps the children broke.
I saw the sheenie-man pissing
into a little paper fire
in the snow, and laughed.
The bird smiled. When I unlatched
the window the bird looked back
three times over each shoulder
then shook his head.
He was never coming back inside,
and rose in a shower
of white dust above
the blazing roofs
and telephone poles.

It meant a child
would have to leave the world.

UNCLE

I remember the forehead born
before Abraham
and flecked with white paint,
the two hands kneading
each other at the sink.
In the basement on Grand
he showed me
his radio,
Manila, Atlantis,
the cities of the burning plains,
the coupons
in comic books, the ads of the air.
Prophet of burned cars
and broken fans, he taught   •
the toilet the eternal,
argued the Talmud
under his nails. The long boats
with the names of winds
set sail
in the sea of his blind eye.

How could he come
humpbacked
in his crisp undershirt
on the front porch in black Detroit
bringing in the milk,
the newspaper, the bills
long past noon? His truck howls
all night to Benton Harbor, Saginaw,
Dog of the Prairie.
In the high work camps
the men break toward dawn.
He sleeps under a mountain.
Uncle, I call you again Uncle,
I come too late
with a bottle of milk
and a chipped cup of Schnapps

to loosen your fever, undo
your arms and legs
so you can rise
above Belle Isle and the Straits,
your clear eye
rid of our rooms forever,
the glass of fat, the blue flame.

1933

My father entered the kingdom of roots
    his head as still as a stone
    (Laid out in black with a white tie
    he blinked
    and I told no one
    except myself over and over)
    laid out long and gray

The hands that stroked my head
    the voice in the dark asking
    he drove the car all the way to the river
      where the ships burned
    he rang with keys and coins
    he knew the animals and their names
      touched the nose of the horse
      and kicked the German dog away
    he brought Ray Estrada from Mexico in his 16th year
      scolded him like a boy, gave him beer money
      and commanded him to lift and push
    he answered to the name father
    he left in October without his hat
    who my mother later said was not much at love
    who answered to the name Father

Father, the world is different in many places
    the old Ford Trimotors are gone to scrap
    the Terraplane turned to snow
    four armies passed over your birthplace
      your house is gone
      all your tall sisters gone
      your fathers
      everyone
    Roosevelt ran again
    you would still be afraid

You would not know me now, I have a son taller than you
 I feel the first night winds catch in the almond
  the plum bend
  and I go in afraid of the death you are
 I climb the tree in the vacant lot
  and leave the fruit untasted
  I stare at the secrets, the small new breasts
  the sparse muff where no one lives
 I blink the cold winds in from the sea
  walking with Teddy, my little one
  squeezing his hand I feel his death
 I find the glacier and wash my face in Arctic dust
 I shit handfuls of earth
 I stand in the spring river pissing at stars
 I see the diamond back at the end of the path
  hissing and rattling
  and will not shoot

The sun is gone, the moon is a slice of hope
 the stars are burned eyes that see
 the wind is the breath of the ocean
 the death of the fish is the allegory
  you slice it open and spill the entrails
  you remove the spine
  the architecture of the breast
  you slap it home
  the oils snap and sizzle
  you live in the world
 you eat all the unknown deeps
 the great sea oaks rise from the floor
 the bears dip their paws in clear streams
  they hug their great matted coats
  and laugh in the voices of girls
 a man drops slowly like brandy or glue

In the cities of the world
    the streets darken with flies
    all the dead fathers fall out of heaven
      and begin again
    the angel of creation is a sparrow in the roadway
    a million ducks out of Ecuador with the names of cities
      settle on the wires
    storks rise slowly pulling the houses after them
    butterflies eat away the eyes of the sun
    the last ashes off the fire of the brain
    the last leavening of snow
    grains of dirt torn from under fingernails and eyes
    you drink these

There is the last darkness burning itself to death
    there are nine women come in the dawn with pitchers
    there is my mother
      a dark child in the schoolyard
      miles from anyone
      she has begun to bleed as her mother did
    there is my brother, the first born, the mild one
      his cold breath fogging the bombsight
    there is the other in his LTD
      he talks to the phone, he strokes his thighs
      he dismisses me
    my mother waits for the horsecart to pass
    my mother prays to become fat and wise
      she becomes fat and wise
    the cat dies and it rains
    the dog groans by the side door
    the old hen flies up in a spasm of gold

My woman gets out of bed in the dark and washes her face
      she goes to the kitchen before we waken
      she picks up a skillet, an egg
      (I dream:
      a man sets out on an inner-tube to Paris
      coming back from dying "the ride aint bad a tall")
      the kids go off to school without socks
      in the rain the worms come out to live
      my father opens the telegram under the moon
         Cousin Philip is dead
         my father stands on the porch in his last summer
         he holds back his tears
         he holds back my tears

Once in childhood the stars held still all night
      the moon swelled like a plum but white and silken
      the last train from Chicago howled through the ghetto
      I came downstairs
      my father sat writing in a great black book
      a pile of letters
      a pile of checks
      (he would pay his debts)
      the moon would die
      the stars jelly
      the sea freeze
      I would be a boy in worn shoes splashing through rain

HOLD ME

The table is cleared of my place
and cannot remember. The bed sags
where I turned to death, the earth fills
my first footsteps, the sun drowns my sight.

A woman turns from the basket
of dried white laundry and sees the room
flooding with the rays of my eyes,
the burning of my hair and tongue.

I enter your bedroom, you look up
in the dark from tying your shoes
and see nothing, your boney shoulders
stiffen and hold, your fingers stop.

Was I dust that I should fall?
Was I silence that the cat heard?
Was I anger the jay swallowed?
The black elm choking on leaves?

In May, like this May, long ago
my tiny Russian Grandpa—the bottle king—
cupped a stained hand under my chin
and ran his comb through my golden hair.

Sweat, black shag, horse turds on the wind,
the last wooden cart rattling down
the alleys, the clop of his great gray mare,
green glass flashing in December sun . . .

I am the eye filled with salt,
his child climbing the rain, we are
all the moon, the one planet, the hand
of five stars flung on the night river.

Philip Levine was born in 1928 in Detroit and was formally educated there, at the public schools and at Wayne University. After a succession of stupid jobs he left the city for good, living in various parts of the country before he settled in Fresno, California, where he now teaches. With his wife and three sons, Mark, John, and Teddy, he recently lived two years in Spain. His books include *On the Edge* (1963), *Not This Pig* (1968), *Pili's Wall* (1971), *Red Dust* (1971), and *They Feed They Lion* (1972).